MAKING LOVE

I0161480

TO THE 50 FT. WOMAN

MAKING LOVE
TO THE 50 FT.
WOMAN

RICK LUPERT

POEMS 1998-2015

Rothco Press • Los Angeles, California

Published by
Rothco Press
5500 Hollywood Blvd., 3rd Floor
Los Angeles, CA 90028

Cover design by Rob Cohen
Cover and Author Photos: Addie Lupert

The author wishes to thank the following publications in which many of the poems in this collection originally appeared: *A Poet is a Poet No Matter How Tall* (For The Love Of Words), *Aim For the Head* (Write Bloody Publishing), *Alternate Lanes Anthology* (Sybaritic Press), *Bank Heavy Press*, *Blue Arc West* (Tebot Bach Press), *Cyclamen and Swords*, *Don't Blame The Ugly Mug Anthology* (Tebot Bach Press), *East/West Magazine*, *East Meets West Anthology*, *Gatsby*, *Get Underground Lummox Journal*, *Men in the Company of Women Anthology* (Edgar & Lenore's Publishing House), *Moongarlic E-Zine*, *Poetic Diversity*, *Prospective Journal*, *Quill and Parchment*, *Radius Lit*, *Rattle*, *Re(Verb)*, *Red Fez*, *Stirring*, *The Bicycle Journal*, *The Blue Jew Yorker*, *The CCAR, Journal*, *The Circle Magazine*, *The Good Things About America* (Write Bloody Publishing), *The Last American Valentine* (Write Bloody Publishing), *The Monday Night Poetry Anthology*, *The Valley Contemporary Poets Anthology*, *Voices Israel*, *We Will Be Shelter* (Write Bloody Publishing), *Yay!LA*

...and probably a handful of others dating back to the early ages of the internet when we were just learning how to remember things.

Rothco Press is a division of Over Easy Media Inc.

ISBN: 978-1-941519-42-4

Electronic ISBN: 978-1-941519-43-1

To Addie, who lets me live the life of a poet,
as long as I keep taking out the trash.

Foreword

A comprehensive selection of Rick Lupert's unselected poetry has finally been realized, thus settling the question, "What are you doing tonight?" What am I doing tonight? I thought I'd stand on a ladder and look down into the pages of 'Making Love to the 50ft Woman,' (2015 ROTHCO Press).

You won't see me in the '10 Items or Less' aisle, with a dozen eggs, shouting "May I please go ahead of you, I just have this one things?" And you won't see me at the miniature golf course, arguing with the grounds keeper about what qualifies as an actual castle. And if anyone's waiting for me to show up at Midnight Forensic Yoga, be prepared to watch the sun come up over your bicycle. I'm busy.

For those of you who know Rick Lupert (and you should at least know who you are), he is a Los Angeles poet with a publishing career spanning twenty years. His work has appeared in many journals, anthologies, websites, and I can think of a few family alters where his work is framed and cherished. He is also the author of 16 previous collections of work, many of them travelogues from years of exploring

If this is your first experience of him (and I'm really starting to hope it is), there is no preparing you. The poems herewith we're written over the last 17 years and represent a fascinating overview of his evolution as an artist. No single style dominates, no hard and fast rule precludes. To ask what he writes about would be like asking a comet, "Where you been?"

I recommend you get your shopping out of the way. Return any calls. Don't bother with social media. When you think about it, most of it isn't that social anyway. No, instead get your comfy clothes on and join me for a spell of 50 ft poetry. Read long into the night if you can. It helps if you actually read to the night, in a soft voice. Say with me "I Like Lions." Say, "Eggs Any Style." Say, "The Absolute Yes of the Weekend."

- Brendan Constantine,
New York 2015

Seven AM Hurrah

A victory parade was held in my neighborhood this morning. It consisted of a man honking his car horn in a joyous manner. Nearby a chainsaw did its thing against celebratory branches. Congratulations I say! After a while they moved on...time is so vague this early in the morning. Where they went, I don't know. The parade route was not made available to me.

I Don't Want to Go Long

Thank you for having me.
I don't want to go too long.
I don't want to overstay my welcome.

I just want to go long enough that our hair falls off.
I only want to go long enough that our hair lying on the floor
	turns grey.

I only want to go long enough that the dinosaurs come back and say
	hey, where is everybody?

I only want to go long enough for Congress to give up and
	just make everything legal and free
	except for murder and violations of personal space.

I only want to go long enough that the taste of me on your tongue
	is visible
	to your neighbors when you go home.
	I want them to smell it.
	I want them to tell you they want to
		make a pie with it.
	I want it to be the centerpiece of your block party.
	That's how long I want to go.

I don't want to go too long.
Just long enough.
Thank you for having me.

The Mystery of the Hole in My Pants

There's a whole in the crotch of my pants
that keeps getting bigger.

Like my pants are Alcatraz and
something is tunneling its way out
a little bit every night.

I could get new pants but
I'd like to see how this plays out.

A Cliche Gone Bad

When the moon hits your eye
like a big pizza pie
it's already too late.

A Morning In the Life

It is just ten a.m. and I am already back in my pajamas
after delivering the child to the preschool and acquiring
the weekly items from the boutique grocery store.

This is how it will be for the rest of the day,
Monday morning, me, in the pajamas, the front door,
not opened again.

When I arrived home I checked in on the social network
which informed me I am now the mayor of my house.
I feel like I stole an election.

My wife asks me what changes am I going to implement
now that I've risen to this power.
Oh, you know... I tell her.

*Probably stay the course...a thousand light bulbs changed
after they burn out. I'll probably bring the troops home
and implement a no gopher policy for the front yard.*

I'm *mad with power* she suggests. At least I think she
would suggest this, if she were home. She's not.
It's Monday morning. I'm just in my pajamas

making stuff up.

Titles of Sad Poems I'm Not Reading Tonight

The Essence of Black Roses

Poem About the Day They Broke Into My House,
Stole All My Stuff and Set Me on Fire

The War In Iraq

Santa Claus Died Yesterday and He Took
The Easter Bunny and Hannukah Harry With Him

The 2000 Presidential Election

My Diseased Ancestors

Photosynthesis Doesn't Work at My House

Science Proves That Chocolate and Love
Cause Death And Sorrow

One Day I Came Home And Found
My Cat Had Eaten Itself

Reasons Why I'm Going To Kill Myself

One Day The Planet Exploded, and We All Died
Especially All the Babies

Who Lives Inside Me?

and how did they get there?
Surely there is a technology
at work here
Who lives inside me?

I know they're there,
I've felt a breakfast meeting
near my spleen,
a rave, just last week

outside one of my
ventricles.
Who lives inside me?
My god, they couldn't possibly

be very tall.
I'm barely allowed on roller coasters
as it is.
Who lives inside me?

Are they even Jewish?
And for heaven's sake
how do they get their mail?

I Like Lions

for Amélie Frank

Once we were all invited to the San Diego Zoo
to write poetry amongst the animals
for an eventual coffee table book
which never came to be

Fuck You Lion Bastard
was the first thing that popped into my head
Like the book, the poem never materialized
Though there are some

who upon greeting me still say
Fuck You Lion Bastard and
so much is communicated
when it is said

Alex Frankel Invented Brendan Constantine

It was an accident
like the discovery of penicillin

he was trying to mix a palm tree
with a 1953 Chevrolet

a cat knocked over a beaker
While Alex was in the bathroom

and out he came
already bald

already
demanding coffee

Rules for Poetry

Never use adjectives
unless you're trying to describe something
and you don't want to do it the hard way

Never use the word 'forever'
It reminds people they're going to die
and the last thing you need is people distracted
by their mortality during your poem

Write what you know
Unless you're a fool, in which case
look to the internet, and write about something there

Avoid vowels
and their angry sister
the letter Y

Avoid cliche
On the other hand...

Learn the difference between
epigraphs
epigrams and
episiotomies

Use as few words as possible
In fact, hand out blank sheets of paper
and tell people it's your finest work

If you ever use the phrase "darkness in my soul"
be prepared for me to come to your house
and kill you

If you're going to write in form, do it right
For example, as I understand it, a haiku
is eight hundred words written while
sitting on a cheesecake

Line breaks are important
but use them carefully, once you've broken a line
its parents will never forgive you
or maybe I'm thinking of Faberge eggs

Finally, go to poetry workshops
sometimes they serve food and
you can't write poetry if you're dead
because you forgot to eat

Summaries of Dreams I've Had

I
A man comes to my apartment
begs me to let him paint the building
He will only charge twenty-three dollars

II
God is a British Soldier
wearing a fuzzy British Soldier hat
who can only appear on movie screens
in desert scenes
where he crushes people like ants

III
Same as previous dream
only instead of God
it's my father

IV
I travel under covered horse drawn wagon
around the entire North American perimeter
It is nineteen seventy five

V
I go to sing at a preschool
After the first measure of every song
the teachers get puzzled looks
and say in unison
"Oh"

VI
I am at school naked
I am at work naked
I am walking down the street naked
Who am I fooling?
I am in my underwear the whole time

VII
My friend Robert gets a fatal hair treatment

VII
I can fly
So I do

Shower Explanations For Cats

I slide open the shower door and there are my two cats
looking at me as if to ask "What the hell were you just doing in there?"

So I explain to them, "You know how you two lick each other to get clean?
Well this" I point to the shower "is like a giant licking machine."

Cleopatra, the older cat, cocks her cat head as if to ask me
"Why don't you get someone else to lick you, and you could
        lick them in return?

I thought that's why you brought home Tigger"
        referring to the younger cat.
So I explain to them "I've been trying to get someone like that.

It's not so easy with us humans. There is no cat-like understanding
that two humans will automatically lick each other when paired off.

You cat's have it easy with your 'Oh. You're another cat.
We will now lick each other.' We humans don't have that."

Cleo cocks her head the other way as if to reply
"Well why don't you lick yourself? I spend most of the day doing that.

Why don't you?" And I again answer her head cocked query
"Cleo, If I could do that, we wouldn't be having this conversation."

Those Who Sow In Tears
Will Reap in Lizards

When our lizard died
you wore black for three days.

In mourning I asked.
Yes you said.

I miss the burial by thirty seconds
while looking for a stone to cover the grave.

It's in the shape of a frog
and because of this you are grateful.

In our living room the empty cage seems
not so empty

the crickets still singing his song.
We go to the pet store to see other lizards.

They are cute like midget dinosaurs
but you, later in the kitchen, weeping

to the chirping of an empty habitat
hold me and say I can't replace my lizard.

I know how you feel.
I look at everything that moves in our house

an essential contrast to stillness
I couldn't do without it.

Animal Hospitality

I can tell which cat is walking through my house
by the sounds its paws make as they come
into contact with the wood floors.

At one in the morning when I finally arrive at my bed
Cleo walks in. She is the oldest cat. Not in the world,
just in the house. You can barely hear her since
    we took her claws

nine years ago. She propels herself to the bed
like a kite. No sound. No bounce. She makes herself.
comfortable. At five in the morning she will purr.

I'd tell you the name of my next cat is Tigger,
but then you would judge me.
He walks in like a pony wearing tap shoes.

If I make even the slightest audible sound or motion
he will rush to the bed and lick any visible skin
of mine he can find. I am okay with this.

Our third cat is larger than a moose. He'd come to
the bed but he can't find room. His breathing is
louder than the president's helicopter.

He will cry for his breakfast with the imperative
of Vietnam. *You're running a zoo* my friend once said
to which I replied. *Let me show you the Chinese*

water dragon and the frog. Did I tell you I tried to keep
a bird alive that I'd found outside? It didn't make it.
Did I tell you about the caterpillar I killed?

Filled Up

for Tigger

Have you ever been so filled with sadness
you literally (and oh, how I hate when people
use the word *literally*, as it's never correct
including now) you literally ran out of room
for your guts?

My cat just died and I'm feeling it.
Look, there's my spleen and both intestines
on the shelf next to the Brautigan.

There's my pancreas and a couple of organs
I can't identify thanks to my lackadaisical
efforts in high school biology, sitting on top of
an anthology of poems written, oddly enough,
in the voice of dogs.

They say time heals all wounds.
(And to hell with anyone would use a cliche
like that in a poem, including me.)

I'm staring at the clock watching it do
what it does; waiting for this sadness to empty out.
It's a slow drain.

Earlier today I found some of his
dried throw-up in the corner of our bedroom.
I didn't have the heart to clean it up,
one of the last physical remnants of
his presence here.

I miss you Tigger.
It'll be like this for a while.

The Absolute Yes of the Weekend

I love Fridays because
it means I can put on new underwear

and by new, I mean clean
To me clean underwear is like a new day

which begins with a Friday of possibilities
and ends in Hollywood

where giant fruit is my spokesperson
and I am the king of the world

A Week in the Life

Wednesday   A mid-day funeral in Northridge
and half the work day is gone.
The meal of consolation
ruins dinner for us.

Thursday   My son discovers he can open the door
of his bedroom. So he does, walks out
into the hallway, calls for us in whispers.
We strongly consider moving.

Friday   I see thirty seconds of Jack Lord on TV
standing in front of a map of Hawaii drawn
on a sheet of plexiglass. It is 1:30 in the morning.
This is all I can take.

Saturday   A conversation with a Rabbi ensues
about which music doesn't belong.
Her premise: the tunes she doesn't like.
The trip to the Zoo is cancelled.

Sunday   A woman in Ocean park reads a
poem describing a homely fish.
I can't think of a single fish I am
attracted to.

Monday   The cats keep us up all night
yelling at each other in their language.
They know about the earthquake on the
east coast. Argue whether to tell us.

Tuesday   At midnight after the poetry reading,
my car separates a family of raccoons
The babies on one side of the street,
their mother on the other, hating me.

Cliches Gone Bad

A spoonful of sugar
will eventually attract flies.

An eye for an eye, a tooth
for a lifetime of poor dental hygiene.

We came, we saw,
we bought stamps.

The early bird
gets less sleep than the other birds.

If you yell *fire* in a crowded room
wolves will eat your sister.

Good things come to those
who have telekinesis.

If you live in a glass house buy some curtains. Do you think
your neighbors want to spend all afternoon looking at your ass?

If at first you don't succeed
kill yourself.

Make love
not lunch.

Take me out to the ball game
and then leave me alone, I hate you.

Rome wasn't built in a day.
Neither was Cleveland.

See no evil. Hear no evil.
Shut the Fuck up.

Hey, you, get off of my,
leg.

Two roads converged in a forest.
I sued the government for not putting up signs.

And they lived happily ever after
except for the three guys who were killed in a boating accident.

There are plenty more fish in the sea
though I'd rather date a woman.

When the moon hits your eye like a big pizza pie
it's already too late.

Call me Ishmael.
No.

All the king's horses, and all the king's men...
and their wives never suspected a thing.

Eggs Any Style

I
The menu said *eggs any style*
so I ordered mine angry
and a little bit surreal

II
Nude and
a little frivolous

Things Brendan's Mother Can Say To Me

Hello.
How do you do?
Do you have my son's hair?

Do you think, one day, we should
get together behind the old oak tree
and have a healing ceremony?

Have I ever told you I like to receive
telephone calls on Wednesday,
just after I'm done with my baking?

The sweet aroma of brownies
helps boost my already pleasant
phone demeanor.

did you see the movie *Starship Troopers?*
If it weren't for me, those giant ants would
have eaten all our brains.

Would you sign my cheeks and hair?
I agree with everything you've ever said
in all of your poems.

I'm getting a masters degree in poetry.
I understand you never finished college.
Perhaps you should apply yourself more.

I live in the mountains with trees and rabbits
and what Brendan doesn't know is
I already have a bear.

Good day.
Good day.
Goodbye.

Cheese Girl

I know a girl who can't eat cheese
once it's congealed.

Halfway through a slice of pizza
and she's done

peeling off the layer of cheese
with the patient disgust of a vicar in mud.

She's not lactose intolerant.
She's just intolerant.

A dairy perfectionist.
Three minutes out of the cow and it's ruined.

Tofurella?
I don't think so.

Cheeze Whiz?
Not in this lifetime.

American?
Fuck you.

I know this girl
She's particular about her cheese.

A regular Dairy Queen.

Next Time Down

Next time down
we'll park the lawnmower on the other side of the mountain
we'll mail celery to Aruba
we'll write poems about writing poems, about writing poems

Next time down
everyone will get a free pen
everyone will get a free shirt
everyone will get a *Free Willy*

Next time down
this will all be recorded for our posterity
this will all be digitized for maximum flexibility
this will all be lost in the mail when
    the only copy is en route to the maker
        the editor
        the jester
        the barber
        the dog

Next time down
I will publish my novel on a grain of rice
I will exist solely on a diet consisting of
    novels written on grains of rice
I will make crayon drawings of the private thoughts
    of Condaleeza Rice

Next time down
there will only be poems *about writing poems,*
    about writing poems
    about writing poems
There will only be poems
We will not speak of these poems again.

Entire Fucking Sausage

Walking down the sidewalk
and there it is
an entire fucking sausage
on the walk
in my path
begging to be reckoned with
entire fucking sausage
still packaged
shrink wrapped
heat sealed
vacuum packed
entire fucking sausage
could eat it off the
One AM Ground
It screams
    open me
    eat me
    I'm clean
    I'm for you!
entire fucking sausage
Show me litter
muck, dirt
used condoms
gum that will stick to my brain
but no, why

entire fucking sausage
during late night walk
back to car
no woman alongside
no Triscuits for late night nosh
no weariness suitable for bed
just sausage,
entire
untouched
on sidewalk
away from all other sausages
alone in a world of
sausage free walkways
bound to be kicked
thrown at car
utilized as taunting device
missed by grocery bag owner
Oh sausage, you
you sausage
entire fucking sausage
I lay my head on the pillow knowing
we are both alone tonight.

The Cutest Leaf In the World

"It's not going to be so cute tomorrow." - waitress

I
In a salad I had recently
I discovered the cutest leaf in the world
I saved its life

> little baby leaf
> wish it had cheeks
> green dimples
> stem arched like a puppy

Public support grew
The leaf toured the world.
Got caricatured on postage
Freed the slaves
> again

This was the cutest leaf in the world
> Enjoy!
> Enjoy!

II
Where do you get leaves as cute as this?
"Inbreeding"
says the waitress.

III
The cutest leaf in the world
misses the Earth
gets existential about photosynthesis
remembers the warmth of the branch

IV
Some people say
The leaf isn't so cute
They are wrong

V
This leaf
when it leaves the room
people wish
it was still in the room

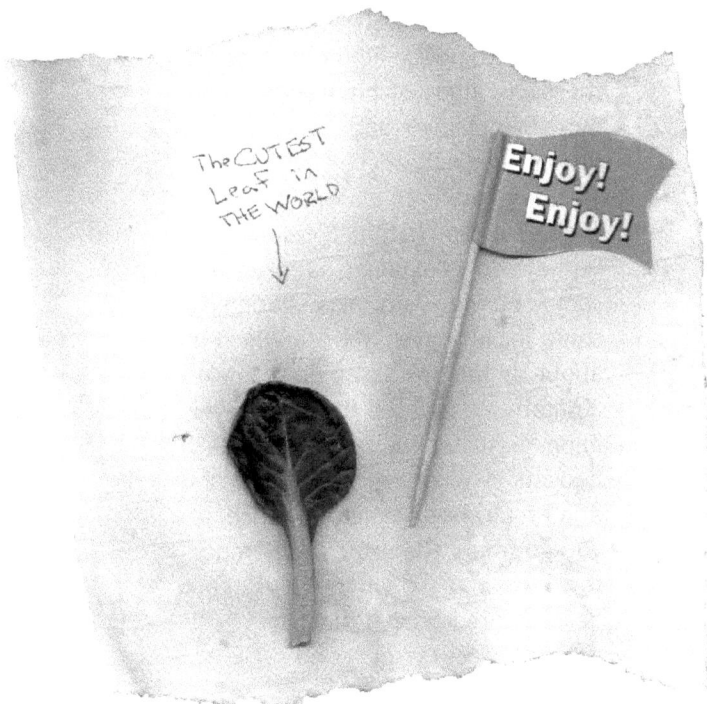

The CUTEST
LeaF in
THE WORLD
↓

Enjoy!
Enjoy!

Lunch, Tuesday

My girlfriend scratch that my fiancee made me tacos this afternoon and I don't mean tacos as in some metaphor for something sexual you sicko perverts I mean the real deal corn tortillas cheese and get this, fake meat and vegan sour cream It was like the SPCA was standing by to make sure no animals were harmed during the preparation of these tacos It was wholesome good eating you demented psycho sexual animals Ate two of them while watching a rerun of Conan O'Brien I think he's real funny but if you watch him enough you start to notice he tends to make the same kinds of physical comedy movements over and over like he doesn't expect anyone would be watching more than two or three shows ever you hateful hateful forest burners Now I'm taking a brake from some boring work like designing some local singers website which is about as tedious as trying to make a database of all the times I've ever been disgusted by someone else's boogars while my own boogars don't really bother me that much do you guys feel the same indifference towards your own boogars you flesh covered boogar machines Best damned tacos I've ever had

This Thought, Too many Syllables for Haiku

The biscuits didn't
turn out as I'd hoped because
too much baking sod

Japanese Day

Today at the Japanese American
National Museum, we were served

expensive tea and complained
that the other table had chocolate

dessert instead of the banana walnut
we were brought.

Today in Japan a wave washed a house away
ten thousand times.

A Good Laugh

Wouldn't it be funny if monsters
attended the poetry readings of
famous poets, and not knowing how
to behave in these circumstances
started killing everyone?

Look there's the Werewolf
gnawing off Billy Collins' ear
while Maya Angelou reads.
Watch out Maya!
Dracula wants your blood.

Making Love to the Fifty Foot Woman

Foreplay takes a week
You have to buy a ladder

When she says *just a little to the left*
you get there by car

You can have her
in two different neighborhoods at once

Mood music
an orchestra

Her bed
a forest

Protection...let's just say
you can get lost in the options

When she finishes
it makes the news

items fall off shelves
bridges collapse

When you finish
she doesn't notice

With a woman so large
feeling inadequate is normal

but she is sweet
makes you comfortable

looks down at you with her eyes
like two Hubble Telescopes

says to you
with open mouth and legs

Don't worry sweetie
You're just the right size

Snake Charmer

for Brendan Constantine

Attention children
Attention children of these woods
Attention children upon whose shoulders
    the world depends
Attention children with scars on your faces
    that tell you've been to the farm
    and back
Attention all of you

Lay down in the forest
Lay down in this place
    few know about
    or dare to come
Lay down by these rocks

When the rattle snakes come
I will make them go away
Rest assured
    no harm to you
    ever

This is my promise
My sacred vow
The foundation
    of my permission
    to be with you
    in this place

So you can go on
    forging the future
with your eyes closed
and your pens in hand

No harm
    ever

Hi Frankenstein

I told one poet
to say *hello* to another

poet we both know
and also to say *hello* to

her husband Frankenstein
I figured she would know what

I was talking about
and if she didn't it would

add a beautiful moment
of strangeness to the world

Werewolf

Those other twenty-nine days
when the moon taunts you
sometimes just a sliver

those twenty-nine days
when you're not on all fours
with flesh in your mouth

when you're not a monster
Do you make friends with the people
see their movies

Talk with them in public like
you think you're people
How about a human girlfriend

Does she wonder
what happens to you that one night
Are you two in sync

Every time there's a full moon
it's her time of the month
doesn't even come over

Never notices the missing clothes
the dirt on your fingers
the guilt in your eyes

Do you eat salads at restaurants
baby greens with a pleasant gorgonzola
For God's sake, how do you pay for it all?

Employment? You?
What if your boss needs you to work that one night?
There's no-one else

What do you do?
He's got a file on you
reads the news

One day, when the moon is big
he'll put it all together
point his human finger at you

Can you already taste this?
Just before the fear takes him
before you open your mouth

he'll get on his knees
beg you
make him live forever

How to Be a Zombie

Forget about the little things.
Now it is only brain
or no brain.

Always be on the lookout for fresh brain.
When no brain is present, try wandering the streets
saying the word *brain* over and over.

You will meet others who agree with you.
You will know them by their smell and
because they will also be saying *brain*.

There will be a discordant harmony to your voices.
Resist the urge to start a barbershop quartet.
Even the living won't be interested.

You may have once loved self-serve frozen yogurt
but now you won't be able to operate the levers.
Let the boy behind the counter do it for you

Then eat his brain.
This is the last shirt you will ever wear.
Don't let the others pull it off you

in the struggle for brain.
Laundry is a concept from your past.
You don't even know what it is anymore.

Get used to walking.
They don't issue licenses to your kind.
There is no special training program and

you'd only eat the DMV employee
when it was your turn in line.
Not that you have anywhere special to be.

Destination based movement is not a priority
for you. Move on or don't. Whatever.
I do not recommend attempting to make a soufflé.

The stiffening of the egg whites requires a patience
you no longer possess. Brains are just as good
right out of the head as they would be in a pie.

Do not eat the dead.
It goes against your personal code
and tastes like shit.

When you run into the living
they will try to hurt you.
They will want to make holes in you.

They will want to make your head
go away from your body.
Avoid this.

When you run into people you knew
it won't matter. You won't remember them.
They may try to reason with you.

Pause for a moment.
Then eat their brains.
Eat their brains so much.

How to Kiss

I
Locate someone other than yourself.
Make sure they have lips.

II
Find out if the person you've located is agreeable to kissing.
You can do this any way you want, except for asking.

III
Make sure you have your lips with you.
Nothing is more embarrassing than moving to kiss someone
and realizing you've left your lips at home or in the car.
Unless you happen to be in the car,
where you can slyly move to adjust the radio,
slapping on your lips during the confusion.

IV
Tell the person their eyes make you want to do gymnastics,
or at least be present where gymnastics are being done.

V
Touch the hand.
Any Hand.
Not your own hand.

VI
Lean your head forward at a slight angle (such as fifteen degrees)
so your foreheads connect first
as if you're attempting a Vulcan mind meld.
If your minds actually begin to meld MILK IT.

VII
Slowly re-angle your head so your lips become parallel with
    his or hers.
Practice this ahead of time using a protractor.

VIII
Allow your lips to make contact with the other lips
BUT DON'T MOVE THEM.
Remain completely still for twenty eight minutes
or until you hear an electronic beeping
indicating it is time to move to step nine.
This time may vary depending on political climate
and lip gloss.

IX
Repeat steps five through eight.

X
Clear your head
so the only thing you can focus on
is a PBS special on *the beaver.*

XI
Begin moving your lips in a slow up and down fashion,
varying with left and right motions every fifteen seconds.

XII
Force your tongue through your subject's lips and teeth.
Fight past their tongue.
Charge forward until you reach the uvula.
Kissing is just an intimate game of *Capture the Uvula.*

XIII
Abandon all tenderness
with reckless nibbling
of anything fleshy you encounter.

XIV
Congratulations!
You are now kissing.

XV
Imagine life as a Frenchman.

Hot Dog Truck

I'm driving westbound on Sherman Way
behind a hot dog truck. This giant cock of meat
I'm tailgating shouts in my face *a hundred
species died to make me.*

It's the ultimate *fuck you* to my vegetarianism.

We pass by a pet store and I blurt out
the window "don't worry guys, I got this one."

I swerve to pull ahead and, sure enough,
the driver is smoking the leg of a zebra.
He's got that look which says
*You want to roll with the wiener you got to
put the jungle in your mouth.*

I want to pull ahead and hit the *fart button*
on my car but then I remember that's
something I made up.

I want to drive on a road free of meat.
I want to put a forest of carrots in my mouth.
I want to wrap my arms around a leopard

so when the credits roll everyone will know
no animals were even looked at funny in
the living of this life.

Oh meat truck
Oh rolling death
Oh *baconalia*

Move aside
Life is rolling by

Zoo on a Mountain

They give birthday presents to the wolves
Three years old today

Wrapped bits of whatever they eat
You pay a few dollars for the privilege

of handing the package to a caretaker
Then watch the pack tear it apart

wrapping paper not of the wild
Happy birthday wolves

I'd like to give you the mountain as a present
I'd like to make the zoo go away

Happy Birthday Hal Sirowitz

Tell your East Coast friend *Happy Birthday*, mother said.
Otherwise he won't say it to you when your birthday comes
and it will create an awkward rift between the two of you.
You need all the friends you can get. Remember
what happened when you gave that boy socks as his gift?
When was the last time you talked to him?

Good Morning Los Angeles

Good morning, Los Angeles.
Our plane lifts off the ground and
circles the ocean.

I wonder if we have enough gas
to make it to Dallas. Our son
points out the window, says

look, I can see the whole world.
For a moment he has me fooled.
We are two hours and twenty one

minutes away from having to
get off this plane and
get on another one.

It is these situations that
remind us, we may never see
our luggage again.

They have not yet made *the announcement*
so we are left without our devices.
A magazine sticky from

someone else's hands.
A catalog with the wonders of the world
only a credit card away.

Is this language not elevated
enough for you? I can see a cloud.
I can see the whole world.

12345 (three)

I
I am driving north on the 101
Cahuenga pass at three am

host to a fog characteristic of somewhere else
or a Hollywood movie.

Closer inspection reveals
it's Caltrans digging up the roads

when I was a boy my mother never let me dig up the roads
these men do it for a living

Do what you love
or die

II
There are seventeen ways to make tea
I only know three of them

I'd tell you but
everyone has to make their own tea

III
You may wonder which
brand of electric toothbrush

is best for you. In the mean time
three of your teeth have left

for the midwest
there's a shortage there

not of teeth, but
every little bit helps

IV
I have five paintings on
my living room walls

three of them
are by you

V
Now here this
You have no control over electricity

The laws of physics apply to you
You'll get three years for breaking

even one of them
Don't do it

Cows on the Freeway

for G. Murray Thomas

My son exists in a perpetual singing of *Old McDonald*
which explains why, after a period of silence,
he'll yell "Cow!" while we're on the freeway.

Expecting me to moo.

Thinking About Eagle Rock

The store doesn't have my soap anymore
so in protest I've been washing myself with wood-chips

and things I scoop out of my cats' ears.
There are those who say my poetry

has lost its humanity. To them I say
Hey baby, have a lollipop.

With a name like *Slaughter*
It's got to be good jam.

I have many fond memories of Eagle Rock.
Like the time I drove through Eagle Rock to get to Pasadena

And the other time I drove through Eagle Rock
to get home from Pasadena

and earlier today when we are at the restaurant.
Remember?

How To Drive to Eagle Rock

At seven thirty in the morning
every morning, when I am
asleep like an eagle rock

you come to wake me
to say goodbye, to say
you love me. Every morning

your smile at seven thirty
is more awake than
I will ever be

I drift back to sleep
your love covering me
like freshly washed sheets

Things I Saw In Echo Park While Waiting For The Little Joy To Open

A locked door
A plaque that read "Billie Jean King"
A place where I could build a shanty town
A dalmatian with a woman
An intersection I had a vague memory of
A woman putting a tree into a truck
Frozen Fish Balls
A package of rice noodles with the word "cock" on it
An Asian woman with a long knife
Galveston Street
McDuff Street
A path to the top of Los Angeles
A man with a bag and no dollar
A stairway to Hell
The letter "A"
A sweet beer
A list of things to be seen
No adjectives

Driving Home From Echo Park

If
I had a key

tonight
is the kind of night

I
would let myself in

piss
in your toilet

rearrange
your watches

Your
tap water

in
my mouth

your
fez

on
my head

If
I had a key tonight

I
would not have to wait

until
Van Nuys to pee

Your
dead landlord

would
not hear a sound

The Entire History of the San Fernando Valley

It is already tomorrow and we are eastbound on Sherman Way
It is possible that we just missed gun shots at Topanga Canyon

Or maybe it was fire crackers in front of the Big Lots
I just returned from Syracuse and boy is my family tired

of my questions about who they are, and where they came from
I wish the Erie Canal had been extended to Sepulveda

I would ship my words to Albany. The future is in mules
We are still eastbound. Some day we will hit Van Nuys Boulevard

which died before I was born, 1968 according to the certificate
but, of course, I mean 1982. Send your flowers to the former

location of the Bob's Big Boy. There will be a meditation
    at Sherman Way
We are sprouting orange groves out of our steering wheels

Earthquake Poem

I remember the day the earth shook.
Would have slept through it if weren't

for the goldfish that landed on my face.
Would have stayed in bed if my roommate

wasn't yelling *get out of the house!*
It was 4:30 in the morning.

4:31 if you want to be exact.
My bookshelf had fallen over.

Would have seen it and not
scraped my leg if it were a reasonable hour.

Restaurants were giving out milk
so it wouldn't spoil.

The kitchen clock stopped working.
read *four thirty one* for years.

The day the freeway broke
The day a hospital fell over

The day we learned all about
how to nail furniture to walls.

This is the occasional price
of living in Paradise.

That Tuesday, the poetry
reading went on.

Windows boarded up.
The one drink minimum

still in effect.

One Night in Van Nuys

Coming home that night
there was a man on his knees
on the sidewalk at Woodley and Saticoy

Another standing over him
couldn't tell if he needed help or
if it was a private ritual

Too scared to roll down my window
at midnight in *this* neighborhood
so I drove the couple of blocks

to my house
where the drought tolerant plants
have grown large

and shield me from the view
of whatever happens
on *my* sidewalk.

Brendan Constantine Receives a Phone Call From My Ass

While examining frozen food
I receive a phone call from you.

Did you just call me?

No.

I just got a call from you on my phone.

I check my phone. It is in my back pocket.

The tightness of my pants caused pressure from my buttock
on the phone's keypad. Somehow your number was dialed.

You received a phone call from my ass.
I tell you this. I tell you my ass called you.

You seem okay with this and, in fact, more comfortable
than you usually do when I call you with my mouth and fingers.

You tell me to tell things to my ass.
You will call it later. I should hug and kiss my ass for you.

You'd talk more, but you are going into a building.
The kind of building where, if they found you were

engaged in a telephone call with my ass
they would want you to end that call immediately.

I let you go into the building.
Me and my ass.

I don't hear from you again.

Drinking Coffee, Waiting for My Wife

It is a Sherman Oaks morning and the plans of eggs
are belayed by keys in a purse in a trunk of a car.

This unexpected siesta at the crossroads of Los Angeles
has more coffee in me than usual. They keep refilling and

I am ready to walk up the side of the building.
Gravity is not my concern. Normally I'm so *straight edge*

at least in terms of chemicals I allow inside me.
I've crossed other kinds of lines.

There should be twelve step programs for people like me.
Hello my name is...and I am nothing in particular worth mentioning.

The phone rings. The keys will soon be where they belong.
A short drive will be followed by an omelette.

It is no longer morning. "Can I warm that up for you?"
"No" I say. They do it anyway. I am obligated to put it in my mouth.

It is no longer morning. My eyes will not close
until the war is over.

Trio of Death

I
That Soup was so good!
How good was it?
Shut up.

II
Rain, rain, go away.
No, really get the fuck
out of here.

III
The best part
about living inside a tree:
Free Sap.

Airplane Money

for Amber Tamblyn and Jeffrey McDaniel

If I were the kind of man who could fly anywhere
I'd come to your reading in New York City.

Page Meets Stage. Both of you have the chops, so
I'm not sure which is which.

I'd come to your reading, but all of my
airplane money goes into my child's mouth.

Instead I'll sit in my house in Van Nuys
with my blow-up poetry dolls

and make believe. Which one of you
wants to be the girl?

Exit Row

Seated in the exit row
we are instructed of our additional responsibilities.
I suggest to my row-mates
that we organize
divide up the tasks
develop a plan
in case the plane goes down.

Someone else can be the leader.
I just want to keep the door
as a souvenir.

No.
Don't hand it to me in here.
Just throw it out of the plane.
I'll get it there.

Strange Birds or These Beaks Were Made for Bockin'

One hundred fifty miles
into Minnesota's snow.

Behind me strange birds nest
on top of Downtown Fargo.

They almost went extinct.
But now they've got jobs

and can resume laying eggs.
There are strange birds in Fargo's houses too.

Talking birds.
Birds that will buy you dinner.

I've got Christian rock blasting
through the frozen prairie.

I'm a Jew,
so you can see the significance.

Somewhere
they're breeding chickens without beaks.

Here I come airport
Take off my shoes

Dallas
John Wayne

Let me eat the potatoes of Minneapolis
Squeeze their lemons

Board a strange bird
Let it fly me home

Today We Bombed The Moon

The good news is
we won.

Lord knows we don't need
another long drawn out conflict.

A few days later Buzz Aldrin
was named honorary

emissary to the moon.
No lie.

How Close Was Mars?

Mars was so close you could see it next
to the moon like they were conjoined.

So close I had to duck when walking up the stairs.
Mars was so close sixty-six thousand years of

history dropped in my late summer bucket like
Los Angeles rain. Mars knocked on my door

last night. Said, in a hurried fashion
"Get the hell out of my way." Mars,

you're so close, the property values are changing.
You want a glass of water, Mars? It's a trick

question. The scientists made me ask it.
Mars, a seed fell off your surface and landed in

our atmosphere. A strange tree sprouted and
grew as tall as a dozen fire hydrants. Mars,

you were so close the new gravity uprooted
that tree and it fell back to you. We're building

a *chunnel* to you Mars. Will you visit? Would
you like some potato chips? Don't answer!

The knowledge would give us an unfair advantage.
Mars, I remember when you were a smidgen,

a twinkle, a *bissel*. A pinpoint of red, just left
of the moon. Just a pinch of you in the sky

giving confidence to the Hungarians. We clutch
our telescopes under our beds Mars

hoping you'll think we're not home. We're out
eating goulash, we're not worth coming so close.

Four Short Poems That I thought I'd Combine Together Into One Because We're Only Doing 5 Poem Sets and I Thought Maybe No-One Would Notice

I
Midgets on a Coffee Break

Billy, Can you reach the creamer?
No

II
Potato Haiku

Don't ever tell me
You're done with the potatoes
If it is not true

III
Midgets In an Elevator

Can you hit number six for me?
No

IV
A Thing I never Thought I'd Hear Myself Say Out-loud

Tigger,
I don't want your anus
on my toes.

Tax Season

I've been trying to write a poem about the men standing in front of
the tax preparers office at Parthenia and Woodley

dressed as the Statue of Liberty for two years. Every day I drive by them
on the way home from dropping my son off at pre-school.

They're holding up a sign that says *Get Fifty Dollars Now* and
spinning it like the marketing department just joined Cirque du Soleil.

I make that sign with my fingers that means either *Satan*, or
    I Love you,
or maybe just Rock and Roll. I'm not sure which.

But I make it every day, hoping they'll notice. It's a hit or miss.
Some days, depending on who's in the costume, they avoid
    eye contact,
obviously thinking this is the kind of person who might orchestrate
    a home invasion.
Other days the sign spinner catches my eye and smiles as big

as a buffalo that's twice the size that buffalos should be.
Yeah he get's it! he thinks. *You know why I'm here.*

And I do. It's only a couple minutes 'til I get home, and as much
    as I want
fifty dollars now, I could just go to the ATM. Plus, I do my taxes online.

But I want them to know I'm okay with them. That I
    remember the time
when I was barely one paycheck away from standing
    on a street corner

dressed as a national landmark, spinning in a circle and hoping for
a bread crumb of acknowledgement. I get it.

I salute you with my Satan fingers, oh human Statue of Liberty.
I love you. Let's rock.

Sex In The Car

I

The car is a good place to lose your virginity.
It's a small confined area
and you'll probably be able to find it
under the passenger seat.

II

The open sun roof
comes in handy
when you're doing it
giraffe style.

III

After sex in the car
I refuse her second offer of water.
"What are you, a camel?" she asks.
"Hump" I answer.

IV

Swinging in the park
after sex in the car.
It's four AM.
Do you know where you are?

Silver

When I bought my car
in the two thousandth year
of somebody else's Lord

The car salesperson
a scrappy middle aged man
pointed to the headlight and said

It's a thing of beauty

I hadn't had a
meaningful relationship in years
possibly ever

So who was I
to assume otherwise?
I named her *Silver*

The car, not the headlight
But to this day when I pass by her front
I wink

get inside and
drive her to wherever the hell
it is I'm going.

It's been twelve years.
A lot of people say I should
get a new car.

And by *a lot of people*
I mean me, and the advertisements
for other cars

which I agree with.
I'd feel like a dirty old man
selling her for a younger model.

No-one else would appreciate
the intricacies of her headlights...
The un-replaced clutch going on

One hundred million miles.
This is the circle of
automobilic life.

I'd tell you more
but I'm now at my destination
and I have to get out of Silver

and do the grocery shopping
so we'll just have to end this
right here.

Winter Haiku

I threw a snow ball
at a guy in New York once
He was not happy

Seasons in L.A.

It is Autumn in L.A. and soon the leaves will come off the trees
Throughout the Southland, a total of six leaves will fall off
    as many trees
and those lucky enough to spot one will reminisce wistfully

about their time spent in the east as a child. Those not from the east
will curse the harshness of L.A.'s winters and continue on their
    long drives
down Sepulveda for destinations as far away as Culver City

I wonder how the onset of Fall will affect the hummingbirds
every day, now that we've installed the feeder, a fleet of the rascals
like feathered helicopters, hovers near the flower shaped receptacles

sipping the sweet nectar I break my fingers every day to afford.
Do they leave town when the thermometer hits the arctic like
sub sixty-five degrees that sends my wool cap on a b-line

straight from the closet to the washing machine for
    its annual refreshening.
Or do they stick it out, hover together for warmth, disguise themselves
as falling leaves, and pray to the bird-gods the nectar doesn't freeze

It is seriously not summer in Los Angeles. Those of us
    with a preference
for cold weather clothes are warming up our credit cards. Fire season
has come and gone. It's time to put out the flood decorations.

I am one of the lucky ones.
A leaf has fallen off my tree.
I watch it drift to the ground like American Beauty

August

"August, die she must..." - Paul Simon

I don't trust August.
After the sweet promise of May.
The deliberate joy of June

The eye-blink of July.
August wants you to trust it
but pretty soon it slaps you in

the face with September.
You're left feeling like a
school boy in heat

wondering where your
summer underwear has
gotten to.

Oh, August
you are a liar.
You pretend to be summer

but you might as well be
the first half of October.
You're a broken down

rail car. You're
rusty and hot, and not
in an attractive way.

I wouldn't recommend
your affections to a homely tree.
Now that I think about it

July, I'm not sure
you're telling me the truth either.
I could swear I saw

you and August holding
hands at the stock exchange.
You're making it so

I go to the store and
the only watermelon left
is a sad one

from the Depression.
I just want it to always be
the third week of June.

I want to still feel
the distant spring on my back.
I want anything that even

looks like a sweater
to be imprisoned in Australia.
Oh, August

you make my face hurt.
my swimming pool melt
My groundhog apologize

for coming out too early.
I don't trust you.
Never have.

Heat

It is nine in the morning and already too hot.
Ninety degrees in the San Fernando Valley

It is truly a *dog day* of summer.
At ten-thirty in the morning it is two hundred degrees.

Hot enough to keep a pie comfortably warm,
so when you are ready, you could scoop

vanilla ice cream on top.
Serve immediately.

At one in the afternoon
it is six hundred degrees.

Hot enough to cook a family of four,
though certain laws request you don't.

At four in the afternoon
most of the Earth's surface has burned away.

I'm writing this underneath the
last remaining palm tree

in a place as far away from the equator
as one could be.

A gaggle of deceased penguins
stares at me wantonly.

Nine o-clock in the evening
I go to bed. It is too hot to be awake anymore.

Probably fifteen hundred degrees.
I'd check the news for tomorrow's potential

but they are gone. I'm going to sleep
until the ice monsters come

until they develop clothing especially for this
until the breaking of the fall.

Haiku - Strip Frank O'Hara

Ever play *Strip Frank
O'Hara?* You read his poems
then take off your clothes.

In Brugge

After watching the movie *In Bruges*
I compared my experience to actually
being *in* Brugge.

There were less guns, of course.
Or was it *more* guns? It's so hard to tell when
you're in a foreign country.

I'll never forget the fat man
from South Africa who put his *viddles*
in our mouths.

Colin Farrell was nowhere to be found.
Or perhaps he's just *that good*.
The belfry to climb up.

The revolution of swans.

Bay Area Day

It is a perfect San Francisco Bay area morning
here in the San Fernando Valley

I would use the phrase *June Gloom*, but it is cliche
and I am against the use of that in poetry.

I am also against the word *cliche*.

The Bay Blend coffee I'm drinking is so dark
It makes black people...

no wait that has the potential to be racist.
It is so dark, half of a zebra started a pride movement.

It is so dark, the moon refused to appear in this poem
because it felt like a poem image whore.

It is so dark, the evil inside me cowered inside my heart
until it thought the danger had passed.

These are the days you want to look out your window
and see a bridge going anywhere.

I've been told using the word *anywhere* in a poem
is inadvisable. So if it makes you feel better

oh publishers of words, oh contest judges
ignore that last line.

In the mean time, which is an unfortunate cliche
and irrelevant since we weren't in the middle

of describing an event, I continue to drink the coffee.
Careful not to say I am *drinking* the coffee

as once in 1990 a visiting college professor told me
to never end words with *ing*.

I am considering redoing this whole thing in five line stanzas.
In the mean time. Shut up.

Have you ever had a morning like this?
I have, though you'll just have to take my words for it.

I'd Rather be in France

Five days away from Paris and all I want to do is
eat French food, drink French wine, wander in
and out of French castles and put my lips on
yours every time we cross a French river.

The truth is, in Paris, if you don't kiss the one
you love every five minutes they exile you to
Belgium. Don't get me wrong, Belgium is great.
It is still Europe. It makes every place in America

look like a chicken shack. But it is no Paris
the city where love was invented, or at least perfected.
The city where the Eiffel Tower is bigger than
you think. The city where if you don't eat a

plate of cheese every day you might as well
kill yourself. I am in Van Nuys, California.
Nine hours away by *aeroplane*. It takes more
to come back. They did it that way on purpose.

So you'd have sufficient time to contemplate
the weight of what you're doing. No man should
leave Paris, not without a solid plan to come back.
If you're a poet and you leave Paris, may the

angels be persuaded to forgive you. Oh *Waterlily*
oh baguette, I've got a hankering for you. Oh Ninth
Bridge oh Sacred Heart. I'm the island in the middle
of you. My lips forever wet with your river.

More Summaries of Dreams I've Had

I

There is a creek of unexpected
alligators

II

Our luggage is missing
When it arrives, it turns out to be
several ketchup packets

The airline employee tells us of the time
she flew to Australia with her mother
naked

III

I find myself in the desert
I realize I'm not supposed to be there
so I twirl around like Wonder Woman in
nineteen seventy six

I trip and wake up

Da Vinci Invented Everything

Machines of war
for the movement of water
air and the idea of love
vegetarianism
vegetation
secret tunnels
the helicopter
wings

Da Vinci invented the kings of France
chocolate bread
castles and drawings
human anatomy
sachets for tea and sugar

Da Vinci invented bumble bees
gave them the idea for honey
He came up with fresh macaroons
napkins that don't come 'til the end of your meal

automatic soap dispensers, hand dryers
the river that runs through your town
Da Vinci invented that

The alleyway
the old church and the clock tower
Looking out over the town from a high place
All his ideas

Da Vinci invented quiche and omelets
pigeons and their eggs.
the places where pigeons live
the messages they carry from
castle to castle

Da Vinci invented caves
the idea of eating meals in them
rental cars with automatic mirrors
exposed beams
the renaissance
Da Vinci invented it all

His own death
The very idea of death and
what you should do before it happens
Da Vinci invented all of this

so the cat sleeping in his bed
at Clos de Luce
told me.

Amboise, France
December 2012

I Am Receiving You From Venice

for Brendan Constantine

I see you have discovered electronic mail in Venice.
I knew it wouldn't take long, after all, it was the Venetians
who invented the internet, except back then it was called *water.*

No one cared about information in those days, it was all about
moving from doorway to doorway in their pointy canoes,
which, back then, they called *gondolas*

Have you found St. Mark's Square yet? How could you not?
Venice would evaporate without it. If you squint there you're likely
to see an Italian amidst the sea of Yankees and future ex-patriots.

These days you can check the computers for digital pictures
of everywhere there is to go. Back then only birds knew the secrets
of rooftops, and they weren't talking.

Today in the square, just one slice of bread will get the pigeons
explaining architecture to you. Be sure to listen. They are the city's
only natives, and they know more than they're letting on.

I imagine you'll walk across the Bridge of Sighs.
When you do, be sure to sigh. If you don't a thousand dead
prisoners would consider it an insult. *You who took*

*the sea for granted, somehow beat the rap with a striped shirted
lawyer. You'll be out in twenty minutes rolling homemade ravioli
down your throat.* You wouldn't want the dead to think that,
    would you?

Ah Venice, as you wander through the paths they wouldn't
    dare call roads
as you see the still life of midnight canals, think of me with
    your electricity
your precise line lengths, your powerful typing fingers.

News of a Strange Thing

for Brendan Constantine

The sweetest message I ever received, was when you called
to tell me you'd seen something strange, and you didn't have
anyone else to tell these kind of things to.

I'm sorry I missed the call, but I want you to know
when I heard the message, I wept my pants.
My role in your life, ever-more defined.

I remember the time you told me you couldn't get
    all your eating done.
I tried, spent a day trying to eat a year's worth of food.
I couldn't get through it, and sure enough the next day I was starving.

Or the time we conceived of a fast food drive-thru for freeways.
You'd order your food at 65 miles an hour by shouting *HAMBURGER*
out the window. Three miles later they'd use a military grade

device to shoot it through your window. Or how about the time I
destroyed a McDonalds by hurling chorizo into the play yard and
yelling *FUCK!* A year later that building was gone.

There's no-one else I could have told that to. And please,
don't get me started about the lasagna that came at midnight.
There have been B movies less successful than the story
    of that lasagna.
So the next time you see a man yelling at a tree on
    Santa Monica Boulevard.
(or whatever street it was, you know how I don't remember things.)
Or you're pretty sure your father just told you he wants to traipse

about New York City with a bag of kittens and a sword, I'm your man.
This is why my ears were invented. This is why I've been
    assigned digits
that make my little blinky box go ringy-ring.

Call me. Tell me what you see.
We'll get through it together.
You sweet sweet man.

My Two Sams

I
I'm convinced that Albert Einstein
    and Mark Twain
are the same person
Maybe it's their accents
or the different centuries they lived in
or (the fact) that I always see them
    in the same room
at the same time
    wherever I go

II
Albert Einstein and Mark Twain
    are spying on me
They've established a residence
    in my peripheral vision
Every few minutes
    I hear a noise

III
I was confronted today by Mark Twain
    and Albert Einstein
They said in unison,
    "Call me Sam"
I think they want my candy

IV
Sam and I
the three of us
took turns today
First Sam
Then me
Then Sam
Then me
"Why do you get an extra turn?"
asked Sam

V
Nuclear powered river boats
That's all they ever talk about

Domestic Imperative

The other day
I had the occasion to
shout across the house

"I'm not wearing pants!"

The doorbell had rung.

It has been made clear to me
I am not to answer the door
without pants.

You're Our Man - A Recent Poem

for Leonard Cohen

When I first came to you, Leonard Cohen,
must have been nineteen eighty six.
Decades after a million million people were already in love with you.
It was like *Everybody Knew*.
I was sitting in a trailer on Arcadia Avenue in the San Gabriel Valley.

My friend, the one who knows, would fill my ears with all the things
he knew I should know. He gave me Jane's Addiction.
He gave me *Harold and Maude*. He gave me *Blue Velvet*,
Bauhaus, the correct positions to put my fingers on frets
which led immediately to calluses and later to the way I
made a living.

And he gave me you.
Seventeen years old and I learned how everything could stop
so I could sit, like a *Bird on a Wire*, in a mood that could
        not be broken.
I spent the next decades trying to seduce whoever was in my house
with The Best of You on permanent rotation
until I fell, *Humbled in Love. Hallelujah!*

For God sakes, Leonard, you're from Canada.
Does anybody know what that really means?
You need a passport to get in, but when you get there
they give you a hug and all the bandaids you could use.

You may be the *Lost Canadian*, Leonard,
but you put Canada on the map.

You invented the concept of melancholy.
Anyone else who thinks they know what melancholy is,
who doesn't have you in mind, is a poseur.

When you look in the dictionary under the word *melancholy*
it bursts into tears of flame weeping you don't already know.
That is the answer to the question *Who by Fire.*

I know a woman who had coffee with you once and now
twenty years later, it's all she ever talks about.

It's the sole item on her resume.
She's going to climb your *Tower of Song*
until the ants carry bits of her away to the queen.

You were the famous Canadian poet long before
you picked up a guitar in public.

I saw the black and white documentary from Canadian TV.
You, a young man, reading your poems to the well-dressed
hipsters of the day.

Your backstage party banter, confident like an educated teenager.
There was no question you could *Take Manhattan.*

No-one thought it was possible your words could
cause more guts to be discombobulated
until you started to strum along with them.
It was like two geniuses got married. *Field Commander Cohen.*
Yes. *This is What We Wanted.*

Your voice started deep and now on the occasion of
    your eightieth birthday
it's so far down they measure it on the richter scale.
It's so far down, we can't help but trip over the *Diamonds in the Mine.*
May we hear it until we *Go No More a-Roving.*
Until the ants take us too.

You make us forget the difference between poetry and music.
Like the ancient Hebrews who spawned us both
who didn't bother coming up with a different word for the two.
Poetry. Music. There is no line.

Leonard,
You're our man.

Happy Birthday.

Hallelujah!

            Hallelujah!

            Hallelujah!

Things My Mother Has Said To Me

Wear a sweater.
Are you dating anyone?

You're going to London? You'd better bring nasal spray
because of the fog. You'll get congested.

I'm writing a book of poetry. It's going to be ten dollars.
They can buy my cookbook too, if they want.

I don't let Habib kiss me on the cheeks because he's a man
and I don't want him to think I'm easy.

Maybe you'll meet a nice girl in London.
I'd love to have grandchildren.

I'm not going to call you on your cell phone because
you might be driving and I don't want you to get in an accident.

I'm sorry I called the police, but I hadn't heard from you in two days
and I thought something had happened.

Do you ever think about having children?
You'll need a girl to do it with.

You should write the Queen before you go to London.
Maybe she'll have you over and show you the palace.

Does your cat masturbate?
Mine does.

Would it kill you to give me grandchildren?
I've already knitted them sweaters.

My Mother Has Another Stroke

My mother lives in Pasadena
and someday, she will be dead.

I am reminded of this as I feed her cat
while she recovers from a stroke.

The doctors teaching her how to walk
and swallow again.

She thinks it's ridiculous
even when they find her on the floor

after she's made her move.
The left side of her body and her brain aren't talking.

It's a trial separation, but as these things go,
reconciliation is unclear.

She hates it when the speech therapist
wraps her hands around her throat during meals

just to feel if she's swallowing right.
They're trying to heal her. She doesn't want any of it.

Somehow she's found cigarettes
and can crawl out to the rehab. wing's terrace to smoke them.

Someday my mother will die
and she won't believe a word of it.

At her funeral, she'll look at us with her dead eyes
and we'll all know what she's thinking

This is ridiculous.

Postcard To Myself in 1979, Syracuse, New York

A few notes to the boy
I didn't leave behind:

After fishing that day on the Erie Canal
don't let the fish drop off the chain

hanging from your bicycle
on the way home.

The image of the live fish breathing
on the sidewalk,

somewhere in the middle of town
will haunt you for years.

Don't even fish.
Just go to the canal and wish them well.

Don't let them put you in the locker.
Don't hit the girl.

Take your clothes off more;
You'll know when.

Don't ask the boy at your birthday party
if he was invited.

Don't go to your best friend's birthday party
with socks as your gift.

You will not have the chance to apologize
for this for thirty years.

This is the first sign your mother
is not well. There will be others.

Burn the golf pants.
DO NOT TRADE YOUR COMIC BOOKS WITH TOMMY NOJAIM.

If it is ever twenty degrees below zero
it is okay to not deliver the newspapers.

Throw them away. No one needs the news
under those conditions anyway.

Whether you like it or not
you are moving to California.

Judaism isn't so bad.
Don't lose your great grandfather's watch.

You will find her.
I'd say, *wish you were here,*

but you will be soon enough.
Far too soon.

Distance Learning

When I drop you off at the airport
you wind your way through the security maze
The physical distance between us becomes incomprehensible

I understand the concept of feet and inches
but what I don't get, is how to move from point A to point B
without your fingers intertwined with mine

or how to eat a meal prepared for one
or how to sleep in a bed twice my size
without you helping balance out the middle

You're the palm to my tree
the headlights to my Corvette
the L to my A

You disappear through a metal detector
Me in the car, on the freeway, over the hill
This Honda was made for two

In my apartment the animals seem content
what the hell do they know?
I see your conditioner in the shower

memories of your wet hair
One day, every day, you'll wait for your turn to rinse off
The California sun will heal your eyes

Our distance will be the exception
and those who sow in tears will reap in the joy of you and I
every night in the same room

Natural Priorities

for Addie

I know how you like to concentrate deeply
when examining produce, and when talking with me

You can't do both at the same time,
or you'll stand frozen and confused

next to a crate of seedless watermelon
wondering what it all means

It makes sense now
the time in bed you yelled out "Mango!"

I won't even tell you what you've shouted to me
in the produce section

My Wife Gets a Massage

My wife just sent me a text message that said
A Chinese man just touched me for an hour and it was awesome!
All I could think of to respond with was
Oh yeah, well I just ate your salad for lunch.
Somehow I don't think we're even.

My Wife is So Beautiful

My wife is so beautiful and she's nice. People tell me all the time, *Your wife is nice* and I tell them, Y*es, she is the nicest person I know and did you notice how beautiful she is* and they usually respond *Oh, Rick, you're so cute,* to which I often respond *Yes, but not as cute as her.* She is cute like baby little girls and unicorns. She is serious cute, the kind of cute you want to shelter with your breath, wear like pajamas to your job. She is cute like miniature ponies wearing bonnets, licking ice cream and cooing like baby, furry anythings. Goddamn my wife is cute.

Entrepeneuse

My wife wants to start a beard cleaning service
she announces Saturday morning as she picks
unmentionables out of mine.

We could set it up right next to your cat service,
she says, *you know, the one in which all the cats
in the world come to you, so you could pet them?*

Before I can respond she says
It probably wouldn't work as she wouldn't want
to touch anyone else's beard.

Caterpillar Poem

Addie discovers another caterpillar
walking up her arm.

We're not sure if they're coming from
the farmers market produce

or if they've set up a civilization
in our house.

Three caterpillars
this week alone

each one found walking up
some part of Addie.

I can't blame them really.
If I were a caterpillar

or any living creature
That's exactly what I'd be doing

Last Words

Driving away rom the cupcake store
which is now also a Mediterranean Grill

I say out-loud
as if no-one else is in the car

I guess it's a lot more lucrative
than just selling cupcakes

then feel a chest pain and realize
these might be the last words I ever say.

I turn to Addie and ask her
what she would do if my last words were

I guess it's a lot more lucrative
than just selling cupcakes?

She says she would compile a chapbook of
my unpublished work, and that would be the title.

I continue to drive, knowing
my legacy is in good hands.

Jewel of Sherman Oaks

for Addie

You are the healthy mushroom of my late Friday afternoon
The kitty kitty kitty sleeping on my stomach
the loofa loofa sponge in the shower

You make it so I can go to Disneyland every day
cook me pasta filled with green protein

You and your comrade take my poetry
and my guitar picks. You glue them together
like art made from crumbled buildings

Your hair and legs
your shakes and noises

You may never take out the garbage
but you shouldn't be co-mingling
with the garbage anyway

You lizard lover
shaker maker
bed spooner

occasional cabinet closer
the heat of my apartment
the Jewel of Sherman Oaks

Evening Flow

for Addie and Eddie Vedder

I come into the room where it is dark
I put my tongue on your eyebrow

You tell me you've finished the book
You tell me we can see the movie now

I say *That's Good* and go into the bathroom
I am in the bathroom with the cat who is waiting for me

You have a wet eyebrow
You have a wet eyebrow in the dark

I do my business
I am sitting near the cat who endears himself to the doorstop

You notice when I open the door
You have bean bags on your eyes

I put my tongue on your other eyebrow
I am aware of the beanbags

You say they help you relax
You and the beanbags and the wet eyebrows

We will see the movie
We, the rhythm of the evening

Eternal Embrace

*Archaeologists in Italy have discovered a couple
buried 5,000 to 6,000 years ago, hugging each other.*

- ROME (Reuters), Tuesday, February 6, 2007

That's the way I want to go
in her arms, teeth intact

Discovered in five thousand years
a beacon to the loveless masses of the future

Our femurs and tibias co-mingled
a love only bones could know

We'll be like black and white movies
an innocent portrayal of a time long gone

They knew how to do it back then, they'll say
just imagine if they still had eyes

New Material

I wanted to call you at five in the morning
to ask if you were mad. "Mad about what"
you would ask. "That I called you at five
in the morning" I'd answer, and then you
really would be mad which wasn't my goal
but at least you'd have another story you
could tell for the rest of our lives.

Familial Costume

My brother in law's wife
which I think makes her
my sister in law in law
dressed as him for Halloween.
Matched every detail.
Clothes. Hair. Stubble.
They went to a party that night
in New York City.
Wowed everyone.
Even hit a number of
Two-for-one specials.
The most interesting part
of the story, I'd imagine,
is later that night when
he found himself alone
with himself.

Haiku

I overhear my
wife tell our four year old we're
all out of eyebrows

New Year Haiku

Careful how you bring
the new year. Come October
a new mouth to feed.

Upon Hearing the Heartbeat of My Unborn Child

They say you're alive now,
getting bigger every day.

At this age, according to the poster
you can already clench your fists.

We hope you don't.
It may seem like the walls are closing in

But trust me, out here
a nice set of walls

will cost you everything.
You have the patience of a seed.

The First Frontier

Jude explores everything with his mouth
I march a baby-safe monkey towards his face
and he is open wide, tongue out, ready to receive it.
Tastes like monkey his crinkled brow tells me.
Later I see him sucking on a giraffe's foot.
This is the second poem I remember
ending with the word *foot*.

Baby Einstein

I see the *Baby Einstein*
series of books on
our son's bookshelf
and I can't wait until
he develops the first
baby nuclear bomb.
It's all relative.

Things My Five and a Half Year Old Said Today

I don't have a head
but I can still talk.

My neck is so long.
Oh no, my neck fell off.

Oh no, all of my necks
fell off.

These two guys died
because I ripped their faces off.

Actually,
they fell off.

I'm making new
heads for them.

They can't be dead
if they have heads.

Dead guys
need heads.

Baby Snot

Because Jude is new to all things
when he gets a cold, we have to use
a special baby siphon, to suck the phlegm
out of his nose.

Oh the things I never knew existed

I wish he could just blow Addie says
and the conversation ends right there.

Discovered Talent

Jude and the Madagascar Hissing Cockroach
have an argument for twenty minutes.
Or it could be a conversation. All we know
is he speaks its language fluently.

Ahh Future Ladies, You're In for a Treat

I gently toss my son in the air because
it's the only way I can get him to laugh

All my 'A' material is lost on him
leave it to a nine-month old to not appreciate dry-wit

So up in the air he goes, laughing
and this one time when he comes down

he sticks his tongue out, like Gene Simmons
below his chin

Like I said in the title
Ahh future ladies, you're in for a treat

The Great Satan

On Easter Sunday the anti-Christ arose within our four year old.
A battlefield of toys strewn about the house.

Intended afternoon clothes anywhere but on the body.
We're pretty sure he took a piss in the middle of his bedroom floor.

We had to take his bear away.
It was that bad.

We were like the American hostages who just wanted to go
      to brunch.
He was like the entire nation of Iran.

Later in the car he proudly announced that
cement trucks could be any color they wanted.

As if nothing had happened! On the road, off the freeway
I saw what looked like a speeding trolley.

Didn't seem safe.

Firsts

Two and a half years of golden curls
litter the floor like an afterthought.

He survives. We all survive.
They say he's still cute.

Of course he is, as another *first*
becomes the past.

These are the unrepeatable memories.
So live in that moment. Seize the lock.

Put it in a jar labeled *first*.
It's all we have left.

Well, there is the kid.
I guess he's got other firsts to come.

Dollars to be received when teeth fall out.
A life to impress us with.

My son's first haircut.
Oh the humanity.

For Pete Seeger

When I came into this world, Pete Seeger
you were already the voice of a generation.

A Weaver, woven into the fabric of America's
conscience.

Look up peace, freedom or pretty cool beards in
the dictionary and there's your picture.

They took you off TV for ten years for speaking your mind.
As if TV meant a damned thing.

You spoke of finding church in the forest. Leave it to you to
find the sacred in a place where there are no lines.

You are the words children from zero to
a hundred and two know without thinking.

You are the flowers that grow out of the ground
picked by young girls every one.

Young girls who will be wooed by young men
who will beat their swords into guitars

and fight their wars with words and music and
a melancholy chord until they too become the flowers.

You showed us this circle.
We have ever learned.

Pete Seeger, your physical body's absence from this world
will never silence your voice.

It has evolved into the DNA of any human who
can see the difference between right and wrong.

We will sing your songs until we too are the flowers.
Pete Seeger, our soundtrack, our spirit,

our conscience.

I Am From Ork

Here's to the crazy one
the one in the red jump suit
the one from the other planet.

Here's to the one who was in my heart
since I knew what TV was.
The one whose recorded words
lived in my house on magnetic tape
since I knew you could purchase recorded words
with your own money.

Here's to the laughter
the man whose zillion words a minute mind
made me a student of comedy
made me hurt like only funny can
made me and a lost generation
fall in love with poetry.

Long before *Dead Poet's Society*
there was your *Martian haiku.*

Here's to the generation who knew you as the genie.
Here's to the one who discovered you as the voice of Vietnam.
Here's to the one who found their Teddy Roosevelt
Here's to the generation who *Naknew* you...

You could be anyone you wanted and
we had no problem believing it.

Remember when your best friend
gave you an Oscar?

Remember when you picked a scarf
out of James Lipton's audience and
did twenty minutes with it?
Unrehearsed, a mind constantly making art.
Who needs an act when you're you?

Here's to you Robin,
head number one on the
Mount Rushmore of laughter.

I hope they bury you upside-down.
I'm going to let my body heal from
decades of side splitting.

I suspect
you've left a permanent mark.
Today we are all from Ork.

The Increasing Finances of Age

Today at the market
an older woman asked to see my ID
in conjunction with the six beers
I'd placed in the shopping cart.

Happily I said, and produced it.
After studying it for a *while*
Oh my god, you're a year older than me!
You Look great!

At first I wanted to bond with her
about high-school in the eighties
Then I felt bad for her, looking older
than her years.

Probably a smoker I thought.
Then I felt bad for me.
Am I really that old?
I collected my beers

and the rest of my groceries.
Over a hundred dollars worth of items.
Back in the eighties, I couldn't
afford any of this.

First Funeral

I went to my first funeral today.
People say I'm lucky when they hear that
to have been shielded from the shock of
our impermanence for so long.

I walked in with a woman who said
My husband's entire family is buried here.
"Apparently Not" I thought.
This is how I deal with the tragedy.

Songs are sung.
The Rabbi speaks.
Children tell the stories
of the life gone by.

We caravan from chapel to grave.
It is so Los Angeles to take
so many cars
so short a distance.

The casket
a simple pine box
a Jewish star on it
is put into the ground.

The holy words are said.
Shovels are lifted.
The widow, fifty seven years with him
is inconsolable.

The cemetery employee
announces the conclusion
collects the prayers in
prearranged black paper bags.

Some go to the meal
some back to work.
We miss the man
are grateful for our breath.

On My Eventual Death

I
Scientists say
our sun will burn out
in three billion years;

all life on earth
that ever was,
gone.

With this in mind
it is my policy to not make
long term plans or

worry too much
about my
legacy.

II
I read about a couple
that had their beloved dog
cloned.

Addie asks if want to clone
my beloved Tigger. I tell her
yes;

because she would love him
as a kitten and so he could
be with us forever.

I tell her it costs
one hundred eighty thousand
dollars

and she screams
doesn't listen to another word
I say.

I tell her I heard the price is
going down, but she doesn't hear me
is still screaming.

III
Knowing my family's history
of heart failure, I ask Addie

If I die young, and you remarry,
which I would understand, would you
agree to be buried next to me.

I hope you have a happy life with the new guy;
but I couldn't imagine spending eternity
under the ground without you.

Addie is, of course, horrified
but she agrees
which comforts me.

IV
Jude, my son
holds his fist in the air
like *fight the power*

as the milk goes into his mouth

Ah Jude, my son,
my little Black Panther
you will outlive us all.

THANK YOU

The author wishes to thank the following publications in which many of the poems in this collection originally appeared:

A Poet is a Poet No Matter How Tall (For The Love Of Words), Aim For the Head (Write Bloody Publishing), Alternate Lanes Anthology (Sybaritic Press), Bank Heavy Press, Blue Arc West (Tebot Bach Press), Cyclamen and Swords, Don't Blame The Ugly Mug Anthology (Tebot Bach Press), East / West Magazine, East Meets West Anthology, Gatsby, Get Underground, Lummox Journal, Men in the Company of Women Anthology (Edgar & Lenore's Publishing House), Moongarlic E-Zine, Poetic Diversity, Prospective Journal, Quill and Parchment, Radius Lit, Rattle, Re(Verb), Red Fez, Stirring, The Bicycle Journal, The Blue Jew Yorker, The Circle Magazine, The Good Things About America (Write Bloody Publishing), The Last American Valentine (Write Bloody Publishing), The Monday Night Poetry Anthology, The Valley Contemporary Poets Anthology, Voices Israel, We Will Be Shelter (Write Bloody Publishing), Yay! LA

...and probably a handful of others dating back to the early ages of the internet when we were just learning how to remember things.

ABOUT THE AUTHOR

Best of the Net and Two-time Pushcart Prize nominee Rick Lupert has been involved in the Los Angeles poetry community since 1990. He was awarded the Beyond Baroque Distinguished Service Award in 2014 for service to the Los Angeles poetry community. He served for two years as a co-director of the Valley Contemporary Poets, a non-profit organization which produces readings and publications out of the San Fernando Valley. His poetry has appeared in numerous magazines and literary journals, including *The Los Angeles Times, Rattle, Chiron Review, Red Fez, Zuzu's Petals, Stirring, The Bicycle Review, Caffeine Magazine, Blue Satellite* and others. He edited the anthologies *A Poet's Siddur, Ekphrastia Gone Wild - Poems Inspired by Art, A Poet's Haggadah: Passover through the Eyes of Poets*, and *The Night Goes on All Night - Noir Inspired Poetry*, and is the author of twenty other books: *God Wrestler (Ain't Got No Press), Donut Famine, Romancing the Blarney Stone, Professor Clown on Parade, The Gettysburg Undress, Nothing in New England is New, Death of a Mauve Bat, Sinzibuckwud!, We Put Things In Our Mouths, Paris: It's The Cheese, I Am My Own Orange County, Mowing Fargo, I'm a Jew. Are You?, Feeding Holy Cats, Stolen Mummies, I'd Like to Bake Your Goods, A Man With No Teeth Serves Us Breakfast* (Ain't Got No Press), *Lizard King of the Laundromat, Brendan Constantine is My Kind of Town* (Inevitable Press) and *Up Liberty's Skirt* (Cassowary Press). He hosted the long running Cobalt Café reading series in Canoga Park for almost 21 years and is regularly featured at venues throughout Southern California. Rick writes the From the Lupertverse blog at JewishJournal.com and the daily web-comic strip Cat and Banana with Brendan Constantine at www.facebook.com/catandbanana. Rick created and maintains the Poetry Super Highway, an online resource and publication for poets (PoetrySuperHighway.com). Currently Rick works as a music teacher at synagogues in Southern California and as a graphic and web designer for anyone who would like to help pay his mortgage.

RICK'S OTHER BOOKS

God Wrestler
Rothco Press ~ August, 2017

Donut Famine
Rothco Press ~ December, 2016

Romancing the Blarney Stone
Rothco Press ~ December, 2016

Professor Clown on Parade
Rothco Press ~ December, 2016

Rick Lupert Live and Dead (Album)
Ain't Got No Press ~ March, 2016

The Gettysburg Undress
Rothco Press ~ May, 2014

Ekphrastia Gone Wild (edited by)
Ain't Got No Press ~ July, 2013

Nothing in New England is New
Ain't Got No Press ~ March, 2013

Death of a Mauve Bat
Ain't Got No Press ~ January, 2012

The Night Goes On All Night
Noir Inspired Poetry (edited by)
Ain't Got No Press ~ November, 2011

Sinzibuckwud!
Ain't Got No Press ~ January, 2011

We Put Things In Our Mouths
Ain't Got No Press ~ January, 2010

A Poet's Haggadah (edited by)
Ain't Got No Press ~ April, 2008

A Man With No Teeth
Serves Us Breakfast
Ain't Got No Press ~ May, 2007

I'd Like to Bake Your Goods
Ain't Got No Press ~ January, 2006

Stolen Mummies
Ain't Got No Press ~ February, 2003

Brendan Constantine is My Kind of Town
Inevitable Press ~ September, 2001

Up Liberty's Skirt
Cassowary Press ~ March, 2001

Feeding Holy Cats
Cassowary Press ~ May, 2000

I'm a Jew, Are You?
Cassowary Press ~ May, 2000

Mowing Fargo
Sacred Beverage Press ~ December, 1998

Lizard King of the Laundromat
The Inevitable Press ~ February, 1998

I Am My Own Orange County
Ain't Got No Press ~ May, 1997

Paris: It's The Cheese
Ain't Got No Press ~ May, 1996

More info at www.PoetrySuperHighway.com